The Sausage Roll

"The Sausage Roll Pantry: A Rollin' Advent
Indulge in the scrumptious world of savoury
Sausage Roll Pantry." This cookbook is your gateway to an array of delectable pastries, where each bite offers a symphony of flavours and textures that will keep you rolling back for more.

Inside "The Sausage Roll Pantry," you'll uncover a diverse collection of recipes that cater to all tastes and occasions. From classic favourites like the traditional pork sausage roll to international inspirations like the fiery Cajun sausage roll, this cookbook is your culinary passport to a world of finger-licking goodness.

Let the comforting aroma of freshly baked sausage rolls fill your kitchen, and the pleasure of biting into a golden, warm pastry melt away your day's stresses. From timeless classics to innovative gourmet twists, "The Sausage Roll Pantry" promises an abundance of inspiration and gratification for your taste buds. It's a cookbook that brings friends and family together, making every occasion a rolling celebration of good food and great company.

So, make "The Sausage Roll Pan pantry" your go-to guide for crafting the perfect sausage rolls, be it for a cozy night in, a picnic, or your next gathering. Roll with it, experiment with flavours, and get ready to be amazed by the world of savoury indulgence that these recipes offer.

Index

Here are 30 sausage roll recipes:

Classic Sausage Rolls:
1. Traditional Sausage Rolls: Classic pork sausage filling wrapped in flaky pastry.
2. Beef Sausage Rolls: Sausage rolls filled with seasoned ground beef.
3. Chicken Sausage Rolls: Sausage rolls featuring ground chicken and herbs.
4. Turkey Sausage Rolls: A lighter alternative using ground turkey.
5. Vegetarian Sausage Rolls: Vegetarian rolls filled with plant-based sausage or vegetables.
6. Spicy Sausage Rolls: Sausage rolls with a kick, using spicy sausage meat.
7. Mini Sausage Rolls: Bite-sized sausage rolls perfect for parties or appetizers.
8. Breakfast Sausage Rolls: Sausage rolls with a breakfast twist, including eggs and cheese.
9. Gluten-Free Sausage Rolls: Sausage rolls with a gluten-free pastry.

International Sausage Rolls:
10. Curry Sausage Rolls: Sausage rolls infused with curry spices.
11. Mediterranean Sausage Rolls: Filling with Mediterranean herbs and spices.
12. Spanish Chorizo Sausage Rolls: Sausage rolls featuring Spanish chorizo.
13. Italian Sausage Rolls: Sausage rolls with Italian sausage and herbs.
14. Mexican Chorizo Sausage Rolls: Spicy sausage rolls inspired by Mexican chorizo.
15. Cajun Sausage Rolls: Sausage rolls with Cajun seasoning for a zesty kick.

16. Greek Sausage Rolls: Filling with Greek flavours like feta cheese and olives.
17. Thai Sausage Rolls: Sausage rolls inspired by Thai cuisine with lemongrass and cilantro.
18. Moroccan Sausage Rolls: Sausage rolls filled with Moroccan spices and dried fruits.
19. Japanese Teriyaki Sausage Rolls: Sausage rolls with a teriyaki twist.

Creative Sausage Rolls:
20. Spinach and Feta Sausage Rolls: A vegetarian option with spinach and feta.
21. Pesto and Sun-Dried Tomato Sausage Rolls: Sausage rolls featuring pesto and sun-dried tomatoes.
22. Blue Cheese and Walnut Sausage Rolls: Sausage rolls with a gourmet twist.
23. Apple and Sage Sausage Rolls: A sweet and savoury combination.
24. Cranberry and Brie Sausage Rolls: Sausage rolls with a holiday flair.
25. Bacon-Wrapped Sausage Rolls: Sausage rolls wrapped in bacon for extra flavour.
26. Maple Glazed Sausage Rolls: Sausage rolls with a sweet maple glaze.
27. Fig and Goat Cheese Sausage Rolls: Sausage rolls with fig and goat cheese.
28. Mashed Potato Sausage Rolls: Sausage rolls with a creamy mashed potato filling.
29. Pizza Sausage Rolls: Sausage rolls inspired by pizza flavours.
30. Vegan Sausage Rolls: Vegan sausage rolls using plant-based sausage.

These sausage roll recipes offer a wide variety of flavours, from classic to international and creative twists, ensuring there's a sausage roll for every palate and occasion.

Enjoy exploring these delicious options!

1. Traditional Sausage Rolls:

Ingredients:
- 500g pork sausage meat
- 1 package puff pastry sheets (thawed if frozen)
- 1 egg (beaten, for egg wash)
- Sesame seeds (optional, for garnish)

Instructions:
1. Preheat the oven to 200°C.
2. Roll out the puff pastry sheets on a lightly floured surface.
3. Divide the sausage meat into portions and shape them into logs.
4. Place a sausage log along the edge of a puff pastry sheet and roll it up, sealing the edge with a bit of beaten egg.
5. Repeat for the remaining sausage meat and pastry.
6. Cut each roll into smaller pieces and place them on a baking sheet.
7. Brush the tops of the rolls with beaten egg and sprinkle with sesame seeds if desired.
8. Bake for 20-25 minutes or until the pastry is golden brown and the sausage is cooked through.
9. Allow to cool slightly before serving.

2. Beef Sausage Rolls:

Ingredients:
- 500g ground beef
- 1 onion, finely chopped
- 1 clove garlic, minced
- 1 teaspoon dried thyme
- Salt and pepper to taste
- 1 package puff pastry sheets (thawed if frozen)
- 1 egg (beaten, for egg wash)

Instructions:
1. Preheat the oven to 200°C.
2. In a pan, sauté the chopped onion and minced garlic until softened. Add ground beef and cook until browned. Season with thyme, salt, and pepper. Allow to cool.
3. Roll out the puff pastry sheets on a lightly floured surface.
4. Spread the beef mixture along the edge of a puff pastry sheet and roll it up, sealing the edge with a bit of beaten egg.
5. Cut the roll into smaller pieces and place them on a baking sheet.
6. Brush the tops of the rolls with beaten egg.
7. Bake for 20-25 minutes or until the pastry is golden brown.
8. Allow to cool slightly before serving.

3. Chicken Sausage Rolls:

Ingredients:
- 500g ground chicken
- 1/2 cup breadcrumbs
- 1 egg
- 2 tablespoons fresh parsley, chopped
- 1 teaspoon dried sage
- Salt and pepper to taste
- 1 package puff pastry sheets (thawed if frozen)
- 1 egg (beaten, for egg wash)

Instructions:
1. Preheat the oven to 200°C.
2. In a bowl, mix together ground chicken, breadcrumbs, egg, parsley, sage, salt, and pepper.
3. Roll out the puff pastry sheets on a lightly floured surface.
4. Spread the chicken mixture along the edge of a puff pastry sheet and roll it up, sealing the edge with a bit of beaten egg.
5. Cut the roll into smaller pieces and place them on a baking sheet.
6. Brush the tops of the rolls with beaten egg.
7. Bake for 20-25 minutes or until the pastry is golden brown and the chicken is cooked through.
8. Allow to cool slightly before serving.

4. Turkey Sausage Rolls:

Ingredients:
- 500g ground turkey
- 1/2 cup oats
- 1 egg
- 1 teaspoon dried thyme
- 1 teaspoon fennel seeds (optional)
- Salt and pepper to taste
- 1 package puff pastry sheets (thawed if frozen)
- 1 egg (beaten, for egg wash)

Instructions:
1. Preheat the oven to 200°C.
2. In a bowl, mix together ground turkey, oats, egg, thyme, fennel seeds (if using), salt, and pepper.
3. Roll out the puff pastry sheets on a lightly floured surface.
4. Spread the turkey mixture along the edge of a puff pastry sheet and roll it up, sealing the edge with a bit of beaten egg.
5. Cut the roll into smaller pieces and place them on a baking sheet.
6. Brush the tops of the rolls with beaten egg.
7. Bake for 20-25 minutes or until the pastry is golden brown and the turkey is cooked through.
8. Allow to cool slightly before serving.

5. Vegetarian Sausage Rolls:

Ingredients:
- 500g plant-based sausage or a mix of finely chopped vegetables (e.g., mushrooms, capsicums, zucchini)
- 1 onion, finely chopped
- 2 cloves garlic, minced
- 1 teaspoon dried thyme
- Salt and pepper to taste
- 1 package puff pastry sheets (thawed if frozen)
- 1 egg (beaten, for egg wash)

Instructions:
1. Preheat the oven to 200°C.
2. In a pan, sauté the chopped onion and minced garlic until softened. Add plant-based sausage or chopped vegetables and cook until tender. Season with thyme, salt, and pepper. Allow to cool.
3. Roll out the puff pastry sheets on a lightly floured surface.
4. Spread the vegetarian sausage or vegetable mixture along the edge of a puff pastry sheet and roll it up, sealing the edge with a bit of beaten egg.
5. Cut the roll into smaller pieces and place them on a baking sheet.
6. Brush the tops of the rolls with beaten egg.
7. Bake for 20-25 minutes or until the pastry is golden brown and the filling is cooked through.
8. Allow to cool slightly before serving.

6. Spicy Sausage Rolls:

Ingredients:
- 500g spicy sausage meat
- 1 package puff pastry sheets (thawed if frozen)
- 1 egg (beaten, for egg wash)
- Hot sauce (optional, for extra heat)

Instructions:
1. Preheat the oven to 200°C.
2. Roll out the puff pastry sheets on a lightly floured surface.
3. Divide the spicy sausage meat into portions.
4. Place a portion of the spicy sausage along the edge of a puff pastry sheet and roll it up, sealing the edge with a bit of beaten egg.
5. Cut the roll into smaller pieces and place them on a baking sheet.
6. Brush the tops of the rolls with beaten egg.
7. If you like extra heat, you can drizzle a bit of hot sauce over the tops before baking.
8. Bake for 20-25 minutes or until the pastry is golden brown and the sausage is cooked through.
9. Allow to cool slightly before serving.

7. Mini Sausage Rolls:

Ingredients:
- 500g sausage meat (pork, beef, or a mix)
- 1 package mini puff pastry sheets (thawed if frozen)
- 1 egg (beaten, for egg wash)

Instructions:
1. Preheat the oven to 200°C.
2. Roll out the mini puff pastry sheets on a lightly floured surface.
3. Divide the sausage meat into small portions.
4. Place a portion of the sausage along the edge of a mini puff pastry sheet and roll it up, sealing the edge with a bit of beaten egg.
5. Place the mini rolls on a baking sheet.
6. Brush the tops of the rolls with beaten egg.
7. Bake for 15-20 minutes or until the pastry is golden brown and the sausage is cooked through.
8. Allow to cool slightly before serving.

8. Breakfast Sausage Rolls:

Ingredients:
- 500g breakfast sausage
- 4 eggs, scrambled
- 1 cup shredded cheddar cheese
- 1 package puff pastry sheets (thawed if frozen)
- 1 egg (beaten, for egg wash)

Instructions:
1. Preheat the oven to 200°C.
2. Cook the breakfast sausage in a pan until browned. Drain excess fat.
3. Roll out the puff pastry sheets on a lightly floured surface.
4. Spread the scrambled eggs and shredded cheddar cheese along the edge of a puff pastry sheet.
5. Place a portion of the cooked breakfast sausage on top.
6. Roll it up, sealing the edge with a bit of beaten egg.
7. Cut the roll into smaller pieces and place them on a baking sheet.
8. Brush the tops of the rolls with beaten egg.
9. Bake for 20-25 minutes or until the pastry is golden brown and the filling is cooked through.
10. Allow to cool slightly before serving.

9. Gluten-Free Sausage Rolls:

Ingredients:
- 500g gluten-free sausage meat
- 1 package gluten-free puff pastry sheets (thawed if frozen)
- 1 egg (beaten, for egg wash)

Instructions:
1. Preheat the oven to 200°C.
2. Roll out the gluten-free puff pastry sheets on a lightly floured surface.
3. Divide the gluten-free sausage meat into portions.
4. Place a portion of the sausage along the edge of a puff pastry sheet and roll it up, sealing the edge with a bit of beaten egg.
5. Cut the roll into smaller pieces and place them on a baking sheet.
6. Brush the tops of the rolls with beaten egg.
7. Bake for 20-25 minutes or until the pastry is golden brown and the sausage is cooked through.
8. Allow to cool slightly before serving.

10. Curry Sausage Rolls:

Ingredients:
- 500g sausage meat
- 1 tablespoon curry powder
- 1 teaspoon ground cumin
- 1 teaspoon ground coriander
- 1 package puff pastry sheets (thawed if frozen)
- 1 egg (beaten, for egg wash)

Instructions:
1. Preheat the oven to 200°C.
2. In a bowl, mix curry powder, ground cumin, and ground coriander into the sausage meat.
3. Roll out the puff pastry sheets on a lightly floured surface.
4. Spread the curry-infused sausage meat along the edge of a puff pastry sheet and roll it up, sealing the edge with a bit of beaten egg.
5. Cut the roll into smaller pieces and place them on a baking sheet.
6. Brush the tops of the rolls with beaten egg.
7. Bake for 20-25 minutes or until the pastry is golden brown and the sausage is cooked through.
8. Allow to cool slightly before serving.

11. Mediterranean Sausage Rolls:

Ingredients:
- 500g sausage meat
- 1 teaspoon dried oregano
- 1 teaspoon dried thyme
- 1 teaspoon dried rosemary
- 1 package puff pastry sheets (thawed if frozen)
- 1 egg (beaten, for egg wash)

Instructions:
1. Preheat the oven to 200°C.
2. In a bowl, mix dried oregano, dried thyme, and dried rosemary into the sausage meat.
3. Roll out the puff pastry sheets on a lightly floured surface.
4. Spread the Mediterranean herb-infused sausage meat along the edge of a puff pastry sheet and roll it up, sealing the edge with a bit of beaten egg.
5. Cut the roll into smaller pieces and place them on a baking sheet.
6. Brush the tops of the rolls with beaten egg.
7. Bake for 20-25 minutes or until the pastry is golden brown and the sausage is cooked through.
8. Allow to cool slightly before serving.

12. Spanish Chorizo Sausage Rolls:

Ingredients:
- 500g Spanish chorizo sausage, casing removed and meat crumbled
- 1 package puff pastry sheets (thawed if frozen)
- 1 egg (beaten, for egg wash)

Instructions:
1. Preheat the oven to 200°C.
2. Roll out the puff pastry sheets on a lightly floured surface.
3. Spread the crumbled Spanish chorizo sausage meat along the edge of a puff pastry sheet and roll it up, sealing the edge with a bit of beaten egg.
4. Cut the roll into smaller pieces and place them on a baking sheet.
5. Brush the tops of the rolls with beaten egg.
6. Bake for 20-25 minutes or until the pastry is golden brown and the chorizo is cooked through.
7. Allow to cool slightly before serving.

13. Italian Sausage Rolls:

Ingredients:
- 500g Italian sausage meat
- 1 teaspoon dried basil
- 1 teaspoon dried oregano
- 1 teaspoon garlic powder
- 1 package puff pastry sheets (thawed if frozen)
- 1 egg (beaten, for egg wash)

Instructions:
1. Preheat the oven to 200°C.
2. In a bowl, mix dried basil, dried oregano, and garlic powder into the Italian sausage meat.
3. Roll out the puff pastry sheets on a lightly floured surface.
4. Spread the Italian herb-infused sausage meat along the edge of a puff pastry sheet and roll it up, sealing the edge with a bit of beaten egg.
5. Cut the roll into smaller pieces and place them on a baking sheet.
6. Brush the tops of the rolls with beaten egg.
7. Bake for 20-25 minutes or until the pastry is golden brown and the sausage is cooked through.
8. Allow to cool slightly before serving.

14. Mexican Chorizo Sausage Rolls:

Ingredients:
- 500g Mexican chorizo sausage, casing removed
- 1 package puff pastry sheets (thawed if frozen)
- 1 cup shredded cheddar cheese
- 1 jalapeño, finely chopped (optional, for extra heat)
- 1 egg (beaten, for egg wash)

Instructions:
1. Preheat the oven to 200°C.
2. Roll out the puff pastry sheets on a lightly floured surface.
3. Spread the crumbled Mexican chorizo sausage along the edge of a puff pastry sheet.
4. Sprinkle shredded cheddar cheese and chopped jalapeño (if using) over the sausage.
5. Roll it up, sealing the edge with a bit of beaten egg.
6. Cut the roll into smaller pieces and place them on a baking sheet.
7. Brush the tops of the rolls with beaten egg.
8. Bake for 20-25 minutes or until the pastry is golden brown and the chorizo is cooked through.
9. Allow to cool slightly before serving.

15. Cajun Sausage Rolls:

Ingredients:
- 500g sausage meat
- 1 tablespoon Cajun seasoning
- 1 package puff pastry sheets (thawed if frozen)
- 1 egg (beaten, for egg wash)

Instructions:
1. Preheat the oven to 200°C.
2. In a bowl, mix Cajun seasoning into the sausage meat.
3. Roll out the puff pastry sheets on a lightly floured surface.
4. Spread the Cajun-seasoned sausage meat along the edge of a puff pastry sheet and roll it up, sealing the edge with a bit of beaten egg.
5. Cut the roll into smaller pieces and place them on a baking sheet.
6. Brush the tops of the rolls with beaten egg.
7. Bake for 20-25 minutes or until the pastry is golden brown and the sausage is cooked through.
8. Allow to cool slightly before serving.

16. Greek Sausage Rolls:

Ingredients:
- 500g sausage meat (pork or lamb)
- 1/2 cup crumbled feta cheese
- 1/4 cup Kalamata olives, chopped
- 1 teaspoon dried oregano
- 1 package puff pastry sheets (thawed if frozen)
- 1 egg (beaten, for egg wash)

Instructions:
1. Preheat the oven to 200°C.
2. In a bowl, mix crumbled feta cheese, chopped Kalamata olives, and dried oregano into the sausage meat.
3. Roll out the puff pastry sheets on a lightly floured surface.
4. Spread the Greek-flavoured sausage meat along the edge of a puff pastry sheet and roll it up, sealing the edge with a bit of beaten egg.
5. Cut the roll into smaller pieces and place them on a baking sheet.
6. Brush the tops of the rolls with beaten egg.
7. Bake for 20-25 minutes or until the pastry is golden brown and the sausage is cooked through.
8. Allow to cool slightly before serving.

17. Thai Sausage Rolls:

Ingredients:
- 500g pork sausage meat
- 2 stalks lemongrass, finely chopped
- 1/4 cup fresh cilantro, chopped
- 1 tablespoon fish sauce
- 1 tablespoon soy sauce
- 1 tablespoon brown sugar
- 1 package puff pastry sheets (thawed if frozen)
- 1 egg (beaten, for egg wash)

Instructions:
1. Preheat the oven to 200°C.
2. In a bowl, mix pork sausage meat, chopped lemongrass, cilantro, fish sauce, soy sauce, and brown sugar.
3. Roll out the puff pastry sheets on a lightly floured surface.
4. Spread the Thai-flavoured sausage meat along the edge of a puff pastry sheet and roll it up, sealing the edge with a bit of beaten egg.
5. Cut the roll into smaller pieces and place them on a baking sheet.
6. Brush the tops of the rolls with beaten egg.
7. Bake for 20-25 minutes or until the pastry is golden brown and the sausage is cooked through.
8. Allow to cool slightly before serving.

18. Moroccan Sausage Rolls:

Ingredients:
- 500g lamb sausage meat
- 1 teaspoon ground cumin
- 1 teaspoon ground coriander
- 1/2 teaspoon ground cinnamon
- 1/4 cup dried apricots, chopped
- 1/4 cup golden raisins
- 1 package puff pastry sheets (thawed if frozen)
- 1 egg (beaten, for egg wash)

Instructions:
1. Preheat the oven to 200°C.
2. In a bowl, mix lamb sausage meat, ground cumin, ground coriander, ground cinnamon, chopped dried apricots, and golden raisins.
3. Roll out the puff pastry sheets on a lightly floured surface.
4. Spread the Moroccan-spiced sausage meat along the edge of a puff pastry sheet and roll it up, sealing the edge with a bit of beaten egg.
5. Cut the roll into smaller pieces and place them on a baking sheet.
6. Brush the tops of the rolls with beaten egg.
7. Bake for 20-25 minutes or until the pastry is golden brown and the sausage is cooked through.
8. Allow to cool slightly before serving.

19. Japanese Teriyaki Sausage Rolls:

Ingredients:
- 500g chicken sausage meat
- 1/4 cup teriyaki sauce
- 2 green onions, finely chopped
- 1 tablespoon sesame seeds
- 1 package puff pastry sheets (thawed if frozen)
- 1 egg (beaten, for egg wash)

Instructions:
1. Preheat the oven to 200°C.
2. In a bowl, mix chicken sausage meat, teriyaki sauce, chopped green onions, and sesame seeds.
3. Roll out the puff pastry sheets on a lightly floured surface.
4. Spread the teriyaki-flavoured sausage meat along the edge of a puff pastry sheet and roll it up, sealing the edge with a bit of beaten egg.
5. Cut the roll into smaller pieces and place them on a baking sheet.
6. Brush the tops of the rolls with beaten egg.
7. Bake for 20-25 minutes or until the pastry is golden brown and the sausage is cooked through.
8. Allow to cool slightly before serving.

20. Spinach and Feta Sausage Rolls:

Ingredients:
- 500g vegetarian sausage or plant-based sausage
- 1 cup fresh spinach, chopped
- 1/2 cup crumbled feta cheese
- 1 package puff pastry sheets (thawed if frozen)
- 1 egg (beaten, for egg wash)

Instructions:
1. Preheat the oven to 200°C.
2. In a bowl, mix vegetarian or plant-based sausage, chopped fresh spinach, and crumbled feta cheese.
3. Roll out the puff pastry sheets on a lightly floured surface.
4. Spread the spinach and feta-flavoured sausage mixture along the edge of a puff pastry sheet and roll it up, sealing the edge with a bit of beaten egg.
5. Cut the roll into smaller pieces and place them on a baking sheet.
6. Brush the tops of the rolls with beaten egg.
7. Bake for 20-25 minutes or until the pastry is golden brown and the sausage is cooked through.
8. Allow to cool slightly before serving.

21. Pesto and Sun-Dried Tomato Sausage Rolls:

Ingredients:
- 500g sausage meat (pork or chicken)
- 2 tablespoons pesto sauce
- 1/4 cup sun-dried tomatoes, chopped
- 1 package puff pastry sheets (thawed if frozen)
- 1 egg (beaten, for egg wash)

Instructions:
1. Preheat the oven to 200°C.
2. In a bowl, mix sausage meat, pesto sauce, and chopped sun-dried tomatoes.
3. Roll out the puff pastry sheets on a lightly floured surface.
4. Spread the pesto and sun-dried tomato-flavoured sausage meat along the edge of a puff pastry sheet and roll it up, sealing the edge with a bit of beaten egg.
5. Cut the roll into smaller pieces and place them on a baking sheet.
6. Brush the tops of the rolls with beaten egg.
7. Bake for 20-25 minutes or until the pastry is golden brown and the sausage is cooked through.
8. Allow to cool slightly before serving.

22. Blue Cheese and Walnut Sausage Rolls:

Ingredients:
- 500g sausage meat (pork or beef)
- 1/2 cup crumbled blue cheese
- 1/4 cup chopped walnuts
- 1 package puff pastry sheets (thawed if frozen)
- 1 egg (beaten, for egg wash)

Instructions:
1. Preheat the oven to 200°C.
2. In a bowl, mix sausage meat, crumbled blue cheese, and chopped walnuts.
3. Roll out the puff pastry sheets on a lightly floured surface.
4. Spread the blue cheese and walnut-flavoured sausage meat along the edge of a puff pastry sheet and roll it up, sealing the edge with a bit of beaten egg.
5. Cut the roll into smaller pieces and place them on a baking sheet.
6. Brush the tops of the rolls with beaten egg.
7. Bake for 20-25 minutes or until the pastry is golden brown and the sausage is cooked through.
8. Allow to cool slightly before serving.

23. Apple and Sage Sausage Rolls:

Ingredients:
- 500g sausage meat (pork or chicken)
- 1 apple, finely chopped
- 1 tablespoon fresh sage, chopped
- 1 tablespoon maple syrup
- 1 package puff pastry sheets (thawed if frozen)
- 1 egg (beaten, for egg wash)

Instructions:
1. Preheat the oven to 200°C.
2. In a bowl, mix sausage meat, chopped apple, chopped fresh sage, and maple syrup.
3. Roll out the puff pastry sheets on a lightly floured surface.
4. Spread the apple and sage-flavoured sausage meat along the edge of a puff pastry sheet and roll it up, sealing the edge with a bit of beaten egg.
5. Cut the roll into smaller pieces and place them on a baking sheet.
6. Brush the tops of the rolls with beaten egg.
7. Bake for 20-25 minutes or until the pastry is golden brown and the sausage is cooked through.
8. Allow to cool slightly before serving.

24. Cranberry and Brie Sausage Rolls:

Ingredients:
- 500g sausage meat (pork or turkey)
- 1/2 cup dried cranberries, chopped
- 1/2 cup Brie cheese, diced
- 1 package puff pastry sheets (thawed if frozen)
- 1 egg (beaten, for egg wash)

Instructions:
1. Preheat the oven to 200°C.
2. In a bowl, mix sausage meat, chopped dried cranberries, and diced Brie cheese.
3. Roll out the puff pastry sheets on a lightly floured surface.
4. Spread the cranberry and Brie-flavoured sausage meat along the edge of a puff pastry sheet and roll it up, sealing the edge with a bit of beaten egg.
5. Cut the roll into smaller pieces and place them on a baking sheet.
6. Brush the tops of the rolls with beaten egg.
7. Bake for 20-25 minutes or until the pastry is golden brown and the sausage is cooked through.
8. Allow to cool slightly before serving.

25. Bacon-Wrapped Sausage Rolls:

Ingredients:
- 500g sausage meat (pork or beef)
- 8 slices of bacon
- 1 package puff pastry sheets (thawed if frozen)
- 1 egg (beaten, for egg wash)

Instructions:
1. Preheat the oven to 200°C.
2. Roll out the puff pastry sheets on a lightly floured surface.
3. Divide the sausage meat into portions.
4. Wrap each portion of sausage with a slice of bacon.
5. Place the bacon-wrapped sausages along the edge of a puff pastry sheet and roll it up, sealing the edge with a bit of beaten egg.
6. Cut the roll into smaller pieces and place them on a baking sheet.
7. Brush the tops of the rolls with beaten egg.
8. Bake for 20-25 minutes or until the pastry is golden brown, and the sausage is cooked through.
9. Allow to cool slightly before serving.

26. Maple Glazed Sausage Rolls:

Ingredients:
- 500g sausage meat (pork or turkey)
- 1/4 cup maple syrup
- 1 tablespoon Dijon mustard
- 1 package puff pastry sheets (thawed if frozen)
- 1 egg (beaten, for egg wash)

Instructions:
1. Preheat the oven to 200°C.
2. In a bowl, mix sausage meat, maple syrup, and Dijon mustard.
3. Roll out the puff pastry sheets on a lightly floured surface.
4. Spread the maple-glazed sausage meat along the edge of a puff pastry sheet and roll it up, sealing the edge with a bit of beaten egg.
5. Cut the roll into smaller pieces and place them on a baking sheet.
6. Brush the tops of the rolls with beaten egg.
7. Bake for 20-25 minutes or until the pastry is golden brown and the sausage is cooked through.
8. Allow to cool slightly before serving.

27. Fig and Goat Cheese Sausage Rolls:

Ingredients:
- 500g sausage meat (pork or chicken)
- 1/2 cup dried figs, chopped
- 1/4 cup goat cheese, crumbled
- 1 package puff pastry sheets (thawed if frozen)
- 1 egg (beaten, for egg wash)

Instructions:
1. Preheat the oven to 200°C.
2. In a bowl, mix sausage meat, chopped dried figs, and crumbled goat cheese.
3. Roll out the puff pastry sheets on a lightly floured surface.
4. Spread the fig and goat cheese-flavoured sausage meat along the edge of a puff pastry sheet and roll it up, sealing the edge with a bit of beaten egg.
5. Cut the roll into smaller pieces and place them on a baking sheet.
6. Brush the tops of the rolls with beaten egg.
7. Bake for 20-25 minutes or until the pastry is golden brown and the sausage is cooked through.
8. Allow to cool slightly before serving.

28. Mashed Potato Sausage Rolls:

Ingredients:
- 500g sausage meat (pork or beef)
- 1 cup mashed potatoes, cooled
- 1/4 cup chives, chopped
- 1 package puff pastry sheets (thawed if frozen)
- 1 egg (beaten, for egg wash)

Instructions:
1. Preheat the oven to 200°C.
2. In a bowl, mix sausage meat, mashed potatoes, and chopped chives.
3. Roll out the puff pastry sheets on a lightly floured surface.
4. Spread the mashed potato-flavoured sausage meat along the edge of a puff pastry sheet and roll it up, sealing the edge with a bit of beaten egg.
5. Cut the roll into smaller pieces and place them on a baking sheet.
6. Brush the tops of the rolls with beaten egg.
7. Bake for 20-25 minutes or until the pastry is golden brown and the sausage is cooked through.
8. Allow to cool slightly before serving.

29. Pizza Sausage Rolls:

Ingredients:
- 500g sausage meat (pork or chicken)
- 1/2 cup pizza sauce
- 1 cup shredded mozzarella cheese
- 1/4 cup pepperoni slices, chopped
- 1 package puff pastry sheets (thawed if frozen)
- 1 egg (beaten, for egg wash)

Instructions:
1. Preheat the oven to 200°C.
2. In a bowl, mix sausage meat, pizza sauce, shredded mozzarella cheese, and chopped pepperoni slices.
3. Roll out the puff pastry sheets on a lightly floured surface.
4. Spread the pizza-flavoured sausage meat along the edge of a puff pastry sheet and roll it up, sealing the edge with a bit of beaten egg.
5. Cut the roll into smaller pieces and place them on a baking sheet.
6. Brush the tops of the rolls with beaten egg.
7. Bake for 20-25 minutes or until the pastry is golden brown and the sausage is cooked through.
8. Allow to cool slightly before serving.

30. Vegan Sausage Rolls:

Ingredients:
- 500g vegan sausage (store-bought or homemade)
- 1 cup mixed vegetables (carrots, peas, corn), finely chopped
- 1/4 cup vegan cheese, shredded (optional)
- 1 package vegan puff pastry sheets (thawed if frozen)
- 1 tablespoon plant-based milk (for brushing)

Instructions:
1. Preheat the oven to 200°C.
2. In a bowl, combine vegan sausage, chopped mixed vegetables, and vegan cheese (if using).
3. Roll out the vegan puff pastry sheets on a lightly floured surface.
4. Spread the vegan sausage mixture along the edge of a puff pastry sheet and roll it up, sealing the edge.
5. Cut the roll into smaller pieces and place them on a baking sheet.
6. Brush the tops of the rolls with plant-based milk.
7. Bake for 20-25 minutes or until the pastry is golden brown and the vegan sausage is cooked through.
8. Allow to cool slightly before serving.

Printed in Great Britain
by Amazon